POCKET BIBLE

on Healing

Scriptures to Renew Your Mind
And Change Your Life

Harrison House
Tulsa, Oklahoma

Introduction

If the bruising and wounds Jesus took at Calvary were for our healing - as well as for our righteousness and prosperity - why are so many Christians sick in their minds and bodies? First Peter 2:24 in The Amplified Bible says, "By His wounds you have been healed." Past tense!

Solomon said God's Word is life and health to the peron who will meditate upon it and not let it depart from his or her eyes or heart. (Proverbs 4:20-22.)

It's time to rise up in your faith - believing and speaking what God says, as opposed to what circumstances dictate - for the resurrection Spirit that is alive in you as a child of God and that is

alive in God's Word is greater than any sickness
or disease. The compliation of healing scriptures
in this Pocket Bible has been made to help you
rise up in your inner man and throw off all of
the oppressive works of the devil (Acts 10:38) by
believing, receiving, confessing, and acting upon
these healing truths.

Truly if you have faith and
don't doubt you can do all things

Jer.   30:17 — 8:22
ʻʼ   33:6
Psalms   107:20

PRAYER

Father, I now understand that it is Your will that I walk in completeness, soundness, and perfect wholeness in my spirit, soul, and body. Jesus Christ, Your Son, and now my Lord and Savior, paid the price in full at Calvary's cross for my health and well-being. I refuse to be robbed of this provision any longer, in Jesus' name.

The alien forces of wrong, thoughts, oppression, depression, torment, fear, affliction, infirmity, sickness, and disease cannot reside in me, because You live in me now, Lord Jesus, through the Person of the Holy Spirit. With the authority You have invested in me, I command every alien force to be replaced by Your resurrection power.

Today, I receive an exchange of Your strength for my weakness; Your joy for my sadness; Your pleasure and delight for my sorrow and heaviness; Your hope for my despair; Your peace for my torment; Your prosperity of spirit, body, mind, finances, and relationships for any lack I have experienced; Your ability for my inability; Your acceptance for my rejection; Your obedience for my rebellion; Your encouragement for my discouragement; Your soundness for my brokenness; Your comfort for my pain; and Your courage, Lord, for my fear and timidity.

I command my muscles, tissues, cells, and blood to come in line now with Your resurrection life, Lord Jesus. Thank You for fully aligning my spirit, body, and mind - and every other area of my life - with Your perfect soundness provided for me through Your shed blood at Calvary, Lord Jesus. Through daily doses of Your Word and meditation upon Your promises, Lord, I will walk in divine health, in Jesus' name. Amen.

HEALING SCRIPTURES
OLD TESTAMENT

He said, "If you will listen carefully to the voice of the LORD your God and do what is right in his sight, obeying his commands and keeping all his decrees, then I will not make you suffer any of the diseases I sent on the Egyptians; for I am the LORD who heals you."

Exodus 15:26 NLT

I, the LORD, am your healer.

Exodus 15:26b NASB

Honor your father and your mother, so that you may live long in the land the LORD your God is giving you.

Exodus 20:12 NIV

So you shall serve the LORD your God, and He will bless your bread and your water. And I will take sickness away from the midst of you.

No one shall suffer miscarriage or be barren in your land; I will fulfill the number of your days.

Exodus 23: 25-26 NKJV

God is not human, that he should lie, not a human being, that he should change his mind. Does he speak and then not act? Does he promise and not fulfill?

Numbers 23:19 NIV

POCKET
BIBLE

So be careful to obey the commands, rules, and laws I give you today. If you pay attention to these laws and obey them carefully, the LORD your God will keep his agreement and show his love to you, as he promised your ancestors. He will love and bless you. He will make the number of your people grow; he will bless you with children. He will bless your fields with good crops and will give you grain, new wine, and oil. He will bless your herds with calves and your flocks with lambs in the land he promised your ancestors he would give you. You will be blessed more than any other people. Every husband and wife will have children, and all your cattle will have calves. The LORD will take away all disease from you; you will not have the terrible diseases that were in Egypt, but he will give them to all the people who hate you.

Deuteronomy 7:11-15 NCV

I call heaven and earth to witness this day against you that I have set before you life and death, the blessings and the curses; therefore choose life, that you and your descendants may live.

And may love the Lord your God, obey His voice, and cling to Him. For He is your life and the length of your days

Deuteronomy 30:19, 20 AMP

For the joy of the LORD is your strength.

Nehemiah 8:10

Be gracious to me, O LORD, for I am pining away; Heal me, O LORD, for my bones are dismayed.

Psalm 6:2 NASB

He asked you for life, and you gave it to him —
length of days, for ever and ever.

Psalm 21:4 NIV

Lord my God, I called to you for help, and you
healed me.

Psalm 30:2 NIV

All you who put your hope in the Lord be
strong and brave.

Psalm 31:24 NCV

Do you want a long, good life?

Then watch your tongue! Keep your lips from
lying.

Psalm 34:12-13 TLB

Is anyone crying for help? God is listening,
ready to rescue you.

If your heart is broken, you'll find God right there; if you're kicked in the gut, he'll help you catch your breath.

Psalm 34:17-18 MSG

People who do what is right may have many problems, but the LORD will solve them all.

He will protect their very bones; not one of them will be broken.

Psalm 34: 19-20 NCV

The LORD sustains them on their sickbed and restores them from their bed of illness.

Psalm 41:3 NIV

God be merciful to us and bless us, and cause His face to shine upon us, *Selah.*

That Your way may be known on earth, Your salvation among all nations.

Psalm 67: 1-2 NKJV

Praise be to the LORD, to God our Savior, who daily bears our burdens.

Psalm 68:19 NIV

Those who live in the shelter of the Most High will find rest in the shadow of the Almighty. This I declare about the LORD: He alone is my refuge, my place of safety; he is my God, and I trust him. For he will rescue you from every trap and protect you from deadly disease.

Psalm 91:1-3 NLT

No evil will conquer you; no plague will come near your home.

For he will order his angels to protect you wherever you go.

They will hold you up with their hands so you won't even hurt your foot on a stone.

You will trample upon lions and cobras; you

will crush fierce lions and serpents under your feet!

The LORD says, "I will rescue those who love me. I will protect those who trust in my name.

When they call on me, I will answer; I will be with them in trouble. I will rescue and honor them.

I will reward them with a long life and give them my salvation."

Psalm 91: 10-16 NLT

Bless the LORD, O my soul, and forget not all his benefits:

Who forgiveth all thine iniquities; who healeth all thy diseases;

Who redeemeth thy life from destruction; who crowneth thee with loving kindness and tender mercies;

Who satisfieth thy mouth with good things; so that thy youth is renewed like the eagle's.

Psalm 103: 2-5

He brought them forth also with silver and gold: and there was not one feeble person among their tribes.

Psalm 105:37

He sent his word, and healed them, and delivered them from their destructions.

Psalm 107:20

He settles the childless woman in her home as a happy mother of children. Praise the Lord.

Psalm 113:9 NIV

I shall not die, but live, and declare the works of the Lord.

Psalm 118:17

I will lift up my eyes to the hills from whence

comes my help?

My help comes from the LORD, who made heaven and earth.

He will not allow your foot to be moved; he who keeps you will not slumber.

Behold, He who keeps Israel shall neither slumber nor sleep.

The LORD is your keeper; the LORD is your shade at your right hand.

The sun shall not strike you by day, nor the moon by night.

The LORD shall preserve you from all evil; he shall preserve your soul.

The LORD shall preserve your going out and your coming in from this time forth, and even forevermore.

Psalm 121:1-8 NKJV

The Lord will perfect that which concerns me.

Psalm 138:8 AMP

He heals the brokenhearted and binds up their wounds [curing their pains and their sorrows].

Psalm 147:3 AMP

My son, do not forget my law, but let your heart keep my commands;

For length of days and long life and peace they will add to you.

Proverbs 3: 1-2 NKJV

Do not be wise in your own eyes; fear the LORD and shun evil.

This will bring health to your body and nourishment to your bones.

Proverbs 3: 7, 8 NIV

With her right hand wisdom offers you a long

life, and with her left hand she gives you riches and honor.

Proverbs 3:16 NCV

My son, give attention to my words; incline your ear to my sayings.

Do not let them depart from your eyes; keep them in the midst of your heart;

For they are life to those who find them, and health to all their flesh.

Proverbs 4:20-22 NKJV

Keep my commands and you will live; guard my teachings as the apple of your eye.

Proverbs 7:2 NIV

Wisdom will multiply your days and add years to your life.

Proverbs 9:11 NLT

The mouth of a good person is a deep, life-giving well.

Proverbs 10:11 MSG

The fear of the LORD prolongs life, but the years of the wicked will be shortened.

Proverbs 10:27 NASB

Truly the righteous attain life, but whoever pursues evil finds death.

Proverbs 11:19 NIV

There is one who speaks like the piercings of a sword, but the tongue of the wise promotes health.

Proverbs 12:18 NKJV

In the way of righteousness is life: and in the pathway thereof there is no death.

Proverbs 12:28

A sound heart is life to the body, but envy is

rottenness to the bones.

Proverbs 14:30 NKJV

A calm and undisturbed mind and heart are the life and health of the body, but envy, jealousy, and wrath are like rottenness of the bones.

Proverbs 14:30 AMP

A wholesome tongue is a tree of life

Proverbs 15:4

Light in a messenger's eyes brings joy to the heart, and good news gives health to the bones.

Proverbs 15:30 NIV

Pleasant words are as an honeycomb, sweet to the soul, and health to the bones.

Proverbs 16:24

Kind words are like honey—enjoyable and

healthful.

Proverbs 16:24 TLB

A cheerful disposition is good for your health; gloom and doom leave you bone-tired.

Proverbs 17:22 MSG

Wise words satisfy like a good meal; the right words bring satisfaction.

The tongue can bring death or life; those who love to talk will reap the consequences.

Proverbs 18:20-21 NLT

You will keep in perfect peace those whose minds are steadfast, because they trust in you.

Trust in the LORD forever, for the LORD, the LORD himself, is the Rock eternal.

Isaiah 26:3-4 NIV

For with stammering lips and another tongue

will he speak to this people.

To whom he said, This is the rest wherewith ye may cause the weary to rest; and this is the refreshing: yet they would not hear.

Isaiah 28:11-12

People will look to the king for help, and they will truly listen to what he says.

People who are now worried will be able to understand. Those who cannot speak clearly now will then be able to speak clearly and quickly.

Isaiah 32:3-4 NCV

Strengthen ye the weak hands, and confirm the feeble knees.

Isaiah 35:3

Then will the eyes of the blind be opened and

the ears of the deaf unstopped.

Isaiah 35:5 NIV

Then will the lame leap like a deer, and the mute tongue shout for joy.

Isaiah 35:6 NIV

He gives strength to the weary and increases the power of the weak.

Even youths grow tired and weary, and young men stumble and fall;

but those who hope in the LORD will renew their strength. They will soar on wings like eagles; they will run and not grow weary, they will walk and not be faint.

Isaiah 40:29-31 NIV

Hear, ye deaf; and look, ye blind, that ye may

see.

Isaiah 42:18

But now, thus says the Lord, your Creator, O Jacob, and He who formed you, O Israel, "Do not fear, for I have redeemed you; I have called you by name; you are Mine!

When you pass through the waters, I will be with you; and through the rivers, they will not overflow you. When you walk through the fire, you will not be scorched, nor will the flame burn you.

Isaiah 43:1-2 NASB

Surely He has borne our griefs and carried our sorrows; yet we esteemed Him stricken, smitten by God, and afflicted.

But He was wounded for our transgressions, he was bruised for our iniquities; the chastisement for our peace was upon Him, and by His stripes we are healed.

Isaiah 53:4-5 NKJV

But in that coming day no weapon turned against you will succeed. You will silence every voice raised up to accuse you. These benefits are enjoyed by the servants of the LORD; their vindication will come from me. I, the LORD, have spoken!

Isaiah 54:17 NLT

So shall My word be that goes forth from My mouth; it shall not return to Me void, but it shall accomplish what I please, and it shall prosper in the thing for which I sent it.

Isaiah 55:11 NKJV

"I have seen his ways, but I will heal him; I will

lead him and restore comfort to him and to his mourners, creating the praise of the lips. peace, peace to him who is far and to him who is near," says the LORD, "and I will heal him."

Isaiah 57: 18-19 NASB

Then shall your light break forth like the morning, and your healing (your restoration and the power of a new life) shall spring forth speedily; your righteousness (your rightness, your justice, and your right relationship with God) shall go before you [conducting you to peace and prosperity], and the glory of the Lord shall be your rear guard.

Isaiah 58:8 AMP

For I am watching to see that my word is fulfilled.

Jeremiah 1:12

"My wayward children," says the LORD, "come

back to me, and I will heal your wayward hearts."

Jeremiah 3:22 NLT

Heal me, O LORD, and I shall be healed; save me, and I shall be saved: for thou art my praise.

for you alone

Jeremiah 17:14

For I know the plans I have for you," declares the LORD, "plans to prosper you and not

to harm you, plans to give you hope and a

future."

Jeremiah 29:11 NIV

"I will bring back your health and heal your injuries," says the LORD.

Jeremiah 30:17 NCV

Nevertheless, I will bring health and healing to

it; I will heal my people and will let them enjoy abundant peace and security.

Jeremiah 33:6 NIV

But I came by and saw you there, helplessly kicking about in your own blood. As you lay there, I said, 'Live!'

Ezekiel 16:6 NLT

I will heal their backsliding, I will love them freely: for mine anger is turned away from him.

Hosea 14:4

Let the weak say, I am strong.

Joel 3:10

For I am the Lᴏʀᴅ, I change not.

Malachi 3:6

"But for you who revere my name, the sun of

righteousness will rise with healing in its rays. And you will go out and frolic like well-fed calves.

Then you will trample on the wicked; they will be ashes under the soles of your feet on the day when I act," says the LORD Almighty.

Malachi 4:2-3 NIV

New Testament

Jesus went throughout Galilee, teaching in their synagogues, proclaiming the good news of the kingdom, and healing every disease and sickness among the people.

News about him spread all over Syria, and people brought to him all who were ill with various diseases, those suffering severe pain, the demon-possessed, those having seizures, and the paralyzed; and he healed them.

Matthew 4:23-24 NIV

And, behold, there came a leper and worshipped him, saying, Lord, if thou wilt, thou canst make me clean.

And Jesus put forth his hand, and touched

him, saying, I will; be thou clean. And immediately his leprosy was cleansed.

Matthew 8:2-3

When Jesus returned to Capernaum, a Roman officer came and pleaded with him,

"Lord, my young servant lies in bed, paralyzed and in terrible pain."

Jesus said, "I will come and heal him."

But the officer said, "Lord, I am not worthy to have you come into my home. Just say the word from where you are, and my servant will be healed.

I know this because I am under the authority of my superior officers, and I have authority over my soldiers. I only need to say, 'Go,' and they go, or 'Come,' and they come. And if I say to my slaves, 'Do this,' they do it."

When Jesus heard this, he was amazed. Turning to those who were following him, he said, "I tell you the truth, I haven't seen faith like this in all Israel!"

Then Jesus said to the Roman officer, "Go back home. Because you believed, it has happened." And the young servant was healed that same hour.

Matthew 8:5-10, 13 NLT

Then on coming into Peter's house Jesus saw that Peter's mother-in-law had been put to bed with a high fever. He touched her hand and the fever left her. And then she got up and began to see to their needs.

Matthew 8:14-15 Phillips

When evening had come, they brought to Him many who were demon-possessed. And He cast out the spirits with a word, and healed all who

were sick,

That it might be fulfilled which was spoken by Isaiah the prophet, saying: "He Himself took our infirmities and bore our sicknesses."

Matthew 8:16-17 NKJV

Some men brought a sick man to him. The man could not move his arms or legs. He was lying on a bed. Jesus saw that they believed he would be healed. So he said to the sick man, `My son, be glad! The wrong things you have done are forgiven.'

The man got up and went home.

Matthew 9:2,7 WE

As Jesus went on from there, two blind men followed him, calling out, "Have mercy on us, Son of David!"

When he had gone indoors, the blind men

came to him, and he asked them, "Do you believe that I am able to do this?" "Yes, Lord," they replied.

Then he touched their eyes and said; "According to your faith let it be done to you";

and their sight was restored. Jesus warned them sternly, "See that no one knows about this."

But they went out and spread the news about him all over that region.

Matthew 9:27-31 NIV

When the two men were leaving, some people brought another man to Jesus. This man could not talk because he had a demon in him.

After Jesus forced the demon to leave the man, he was able to speak.

Matthew 9:32,33 NCV

And Jesus went about all the cities and villages,

teaching in their synagogues, and preaching the gospel of the kingdom, and healing every sickness and every disease among the people.

Matthew 9:35

Jesus called his twelve disciples to him and gave them authority to drive out impure spirits and to heal every disease and sickness.

"As you go, proclaim this message: 'The kingdom of heaven has come near'.

Heal the sick, raise the dead, cleanse those who have leprosy, drive out demons. Freely you have received; freely give."

Matthew 10: 1,7,8 NIV

Jesus gave them this reply, "Go and tell John what you see and hear—that blind men are recovering their sight, cripples are walking, lepers being healed, the deaf hearing, the dead being brought to life and the good news is being given to those in need."

Matthew 11: 4-5 Phillips

Are you tired? Worn out? Burned out on religion? Come to me. Get away with me and you'll recover your life. I'll show you how to take a real rest. Walk with me and work with me—watch how I do it. Learn the unforced rhythms of grace. I won't lay anything heavy or ill-fitting on you. Keep company with me and you'll learn to live freely and lightly.

Matthew 11:28-30 MSG

Going on from that place, he went into their synagogue,

and a man with a shriveled hand was there. Looking for a reason to bring charges against

Jesus, they asked him, "Is it lawful to heal on the Sabbath?"

He said to them, "If any of you has a sheep and it falls into a pit on the Sabbath, will you not take hold of it and lift it out?

How much more valuable is a person than a sheep! Therefore it is lawful to do good on the Sabbath."

Then he said to the man, "Stretch out your hand." So he stretched it out and it was completely restored, just as sound as the other.

Matthew 12:9-13 NIV

Many people followed him. He healed all the sick among them.

Matthew 12:15 NLT

Then one was brought to Him who was demon-possessed, blind and mute; and He healed him, so that the blind and mute man both spoke and saw.

Matthew 12:22 NKJV

And Jesus went forth, and saw a great multitude, and was moved with compassion toward them, and he healed their sick.

Matthew 14:14

When they had crossed over, they came to the land of Gennesaret.

And when the men of that place recognized Him, they sent out into all that surrounding region, brought to Him all who were sick,

and begged Him that they might only touch

the hem of His garment. And as many as touched

it were made perfectly well.

Matthew 14:34-36 NKJV

A Gentile woman who lived there came to him, pleading, "Have mercy on me, O Lord, Son of David! For my daughter is possessed by a demon that torments her severely."

But Jesus gave her no reply, not even a word. Then his disciples urged him to send her away. "Tell her to go away," they said. "She is bothering us with all her begging."

Then Jesus said to the woman, "I was sent only to help God's lost sheep—the people of Israel."

But she came and worshiped him, pleading again, "Lord, help me!"

Jesus responded, "It isn't right to take food from the children and throw it to the dogs."

She replied, "That's true, Lord, but even dogs are allowed to eat the scraps that fall beneath their masters' table."

"Dear woman," Jesus said to her, "your faith is great. Your request is granted." And her daughter was instantly healed.

Matthew 15:22-28 NLT

After leaving there, Jesus went along the shore of Lake Galilee. He went up on a hill and sat there.

Great crowds came to Jesus, bringing with them the lame, the blind, the crippled, those who could not speak, and many others. They put them at Jesus' feet, and he healed them.

The crowd was amazed when they saw that people who could not speak before were now able to speak. The crippled were made strong.

The lame could walk, and the blind could see.

And they praised the God of Israel for this.

Matthew 15:29-31 NCV

When they returned to the crowds again a man came and knelt in front of Jesus. "Lord, do have pity on my son," he said, "for he is a lunatic and is in a terrible state. He is always falling into the fire or into the water. I did bring him to your disciples but they couldn't cure him."

You really are an unbelieving and difficult people," Jesus returned. "How long must I be with you, and how long must I put up with you? Bring him here to me!"

Then Jesus reprimanded the evil spirit and it went out of the boy, who was cured from that moment.

Afterwards the disciples approached Jesus privately and asked, "Why weren't we able to get rid of it?"

POCKET
BIBLE

"Because you have so little faith," replied Jesus. "I assure you that if you have as much faith as a grain of mustard-seed you can say to this hill, 'Up you get and move over there!' and it will move—you will find nothing is impossible. However, this kind does not go out except by prayer and fasting."

Matthew 17:14-21 Phillips

"Truly I tell you, whatever you bind on earth will be bound in heaven, and whatever you loose on earth will be loosed in heaven.

Again, truly I tell you that if two of you on earth agree about anything they ask for, it will be done for them by my Father in heaven.

For where two or three gather in my name, there am I with them."

Matthew 18:18-20 NIV

After Jesus said all these things, he left Galilee

and went into the area of Judea on the other side of the Jordan River.

Large crowds followed him, and he healed them there.

Matthew 19:1-2 NCV

And as they departed from Jericho, a great multitude followed him.

And, behold, two blind men sitting by the way side, when they heard that Jesus passed by, cried out, saying, Have mercy on us, O Lord, thou son of David.

And the multitude rebuked them, because they should hold their peace: but they cried the more, saying, Have mercy on us, O Lord, thou son of David.

And Jesus stood still, and called them, and said, What will ye that I shall do unto you?

They say unto him, Lord, that our eyes may be

opened.

So Jesus had compassion on them, and touched their eyes: and immediately their eyes received sight, and they followed him.

Matthew 20:29-34

And the blind and the lame came to him in the temple; and he healed them.

Matthew 21:14

Simon's mother-in-law was in bed with a fever, and they immediately told Jesus about her.

So he went to her, took her hand and helped her up. The fever left her and she began to wait on them.

Mark 1: 30-31 NIV

When evening came, after the sun had set, they

began bringing to Him all who were ill and those who were demon-possessed.

And the whole city had gathered at the door.

And He healed many who were ill with various diseases, and cast out many demons; and He was not permitting the demons to speak, because they knew who He was.

Mark 1:32-34 NASB

When Jesus returned to Capernaum several days later, the news spread quickly that he was back home.

Soon the house where he was staying was so packed with visitors that there was no more room, even outside the door. While he was preaching God's word to them,

four men arrived carrying a paralyzed man on

a mat.

They couldn't bring him to Jesus because of the crowd, so they dug a hole through the roof above his head. Then they lowered the man on his mat, right down in front of Jesus.

Seeing their faith, Jesus said to the paralyzed man, "My child, your sins are forgiven."

But some of the teachers of religious law who were sitting there thought to themselves,

"What is he saying? This is blasphemy! Only God can forgive sins!"

Jesus knew immediately what they were thinking, so he asked them, "Why do you question this in your hearts?

Is it easier to say to the paralyzed man 'Your sins are forgiven,' or 'Stand up, pick up your mat, and walk'?

So I will prove to you that the Son of Man has the authority on earth to forgive sins." Then Jesus

turned to the paralyzed man and said,

"Stand up, pick up your mat, and go home!"

And the man jumped up, grabbed his mat, and walked out through the stunned onlookers.

They were all amazed and praised God, exclaiming, "We've never seen anything like this before!"

Mark 2:1-12 NLT

Jesus went into the meeting house again. A man was there whose right hand was thin and weak.

The Pharisees watched Jesus to see if he would heal the man on the Sabbath day. They wanted to find something wrong about Jesus.

He spoke to the man whose hand was thin and weak. He said, `Stand here.'

Then he spoke to the Pharisees. He said, `Is it right to do good things on the Sabbath day or to do wrong things? Is it right to heal people so they will live, or to let them die?' But the Pharisees said nothing.

Jesus was angry as he looked at them. And he was sad that their hearts were so hard. Then he said to the man, `Hold out your hand.' The man did so, and it was made well like the other hand.

Mark 3:1-5 WE

So they arrived on the other side of the lake in the country of the Gerasenes. As Jesus was getting out of the boat, a man in the grip of an evil spirit rushed to meet him from among the tombs where he was living. It was no longer possible for any human being to restrain him even with a chain. Indeed he had frequently been secured with fetters and lengths of chain, but he had simply snapped the chains and broken the fetters in pieces. No one could do anything with him. All through the night as well as in the day-time he screamed among the tombs and on the hill-side, and cut himself with stones. Now, as soon as he saw Jesus in the distance, he ran and knelt before him, yelling at the top of his voice, "What have you got to do with me, Jesus, Son of the most high God? For God's sake, don't torture me!"

For Jesus had already said, "Come out of this man, you evil spirit!"

Then he asked him, "What is your name?" "My name is legion," he replied, "for there are many of us." Then he begged and prayed him not to send "them" out of the country.

A large herd of pigs was grazing there on the hill-side, and the evil spirits implored him, "Send us over to the pigs and we'll get into them!"

So Jesus allowed them to do this, and they came out of the man, and made off and went into the pigs. The whole herd of about two thousand stampeded down the cliff into the lake and was drowned. The swineherds took to their heels and spread their story in the city and all over the countryside. Then the people came to see what had happened. As they approached Jesus, they saw the man who had been devil-possessed sitting there properly clothed and perfectly sane—the same man who had been possessed by "legion"—and they were really frightened. Those who had seen the incident told them what had happened to the devil-possessed man and about the disaster to the pigs. Then they began to implore Jesus to leave their district. As he was embarking on the small boat, the man who had been possessed begged that he might go with him. But Jesus would not allow this. "Go home to your own people," he told him, "And tell them what the Lord has done for you, and how kind he has been to you!"

So the man went off and began to spread throughout the Ten Towns the story of what Jesus had done for him. And they were all simply amazed.

Mark 5:1-20 Phillips

And a certain woman, which had an issue of blood twelve years,

and had suffered many things of many physicians, and had spent all that she had, and was nothing bettered, but rather grew worse,

when she had heard of Jesus, came in the press behind, and touched his garment.

For she said, If I may touch but his clothes, I shall be whole.

And straightway the fountain of her blood was dried up; and she felt in her body that she was healed of that plague.

And Jesus, immediately knowing in himself that virtue had gone out of him, turned him about in the press, and said, Who touched my clothes?

Mark 5:25-30

They beached the boat at Gennesaret and tied up at the landing. As soon as they got out of the boat, word got around fast. People ran this way and that, bringing their sick on stretchers to where they heard he was.

Wherever he went, village or town or country crossroads, they brought their sick to the marketplace and begged him to let them touch the edge of his coat—that's all. And whoever touched him became well.

Mark 6:53-56 MSG

Then Jesus left the area around Tyre and went

through Sidon to Lake Galilee, to the area of the Ten Towns.

While he was there, some people brought a man to him who was deaf and could not talk plainly. The people begged Jesus to put his hand on the man to heal him.

Jesus led the man away from the crowd, by himself. He put his fingers in the man's ears and then spit and touched the man's tongue.

Looking up to heaven, he sighed and said to the man, "Ephphatha!" (This means, "Be opened.")

Instantly the man was able to hear and to use his tongue so that he spoke clearly.

Mark 7:31-35 NCV

They came to Bethsaida, and some people

brought a blind man and begged Jesus to touch him.

He took the blind man by the hand and led him outside the village. When he had spit on the man's eyes and put his hands on him, Jesus asked, "Do you see anything?"

He looked up and said, "I see people; they look like trees walking around."

Once more Jesus put his hands on the man's eyes. Then his eyes were opened, his sight was restored, and he saw everything clearly.

Mark 8:22-25 NIV

Then one of the crowd answered and said, "Teacher, I brought You my son, who has a mute spirit.

And wherever it seizes him, it throws him down; he foams at the mouth, gnashes his teeth, and becomes rigid. So I spoke to Your disciples, that they should cast it out, but they could not."

He answered him and said, "O faithless generation, how long shall I be with you? How long shall I bear with you? Bring him to Me."

Then they brought him to Him. And when he saw Him, immediately the spirit convulsed him, and he fell on the ground and wallowed, foaming at the mouth.

So He asked his father, "How long has this been happening to him?" And he said, "From childhood.

And often he has thrown him both into the fire and into the water to destroy him. But if You can do anything, have compassion on us and help us."

Jesus said to him, "If you can believe, all things are possible to him who believes."

Immediately the father of the child cried out

and said with tears, "Lord, I believe; help my unbelief!"

When Jesus saw that the people came running together, He rebuked the unclean spirit, saying to it: "Deaf and dumb spirit, I command you, come out of him and enter him no more!"

Then the spirit cried out, convulsed him greatly, and came out of him. And he became as one dead, so that many said, "He is dead."

But Jesus took him by the hand and lifted him up, and he arose.

And when He had come into the house, His disciples asked Him privately, "Why could we not cast it out?"

So He said to them, "This kind can come out by nothing but prayer and fasting."

Mark 9:17-29 NKJV

Then they came to Jericho. As Jesus and his

disciples, together with a large crowd, were leaving the city, a blind man, Bartimaeus (which means "son of Timaeus"), was sitting by the roadside begging.

When he heard that it was Jesus of Nazareth, he began to shout, "Jesus, Son of David, have mercy on me!"

Many rebuked him and told him to be quiet, but he shouted all the more, "Son of David, have mercy on me!"

Jesus stopped and said, "Call him."

So they called to the blind man, "Cheer up! On your feet! He's calling you."

Throwing his cloak aside, he jumped to his feet and came to Jesus.

"What do you want me to do for you?" Jesus asked him. The blind man said, "Rabbi, I want to see."

"Go," said Jesus, "your faith has healed you."

Immediately he received his sight and followed Jesus along the road.

Mark 10:46-52 NIV

Jesus answered, "Have faith in God.

I tell you the truth, you can say to this mountain, 'Go, fall into the sea.' And if you have no doubts in your mind and believe that what you say will happen, God will do it for you.

So I tell you to believe that you have received the things you ask for in prayer, and God will give them to you.

When you are praying, if you are angry with someone, forgive him so that your Father in heaven will also forgive your sins.

Mark 11:22-25 NCV

I tell you the truth, you can say to this mountain, 'May you be lifted up and thrown into the sea,' and it will happen. But you must really believe it will happen and have no doubt in your heart.

I tell you, you can pray for anything, and if you believe that you've received it, it will be yours.

Mark 11:23-24 NLT

These signs will be with those who believe. They will drive bad spirits out of people by using my name. They will speak new languages.

They will take up snakes. If they drink poison, it will not make them sick. They will put their hands on sick people and sick people will get well again.

Mark 16:17-18 WE

For with God nothing shall be impossible.

Luke 1:37

For no promise of God can fail to be fulfilled.

Luke 1:37 Phillips

The Spirit of the Lord is upon me, because he hath anointed me to preach the gospel to the poor; he hath sent me to heal the brokenhearted, to preach deliverance to the captives, and recovering of sight to the blind, to set at liberty them that are bruised,

to preach the acceptable year of the Lord.

Luke 4:18-19

After leaving the synagogue that day, Jesus went to Simon's home, where he found Simon's mother-in-law very sick with a high fever. "Please heal her," everyone begged.

Standing at her bedside, he rebuked the fever,

and it left her. And she got up at once and pre-
pared a meal for them.

Luke 4:38-29 NLT

When the sun went down, the people brought
those who were sick to Jesus. Putting his hands
on each sick person, he healed every one of
them.

Luke 4:40 NCV

Then, as the sun was setting, all those who
had friends suffering from every kind of disease
brought them to Jesus and he laid his hands on
each one of them separately and healed them.
Evil spirits came out of many of these people,
shouting, "You are the Son of God!" But he spoke
sharply to them and would not allow them to say

any more, for they knew perfectly well that he

was Christ.

Luke 4:40-41 Phillips

In one of the villages, Jesus met a man with an advanced case of leprosy. When the man saw Jesus, he bowed with his face to the ground, begging to be healed. "Lord," he said, "if you are willing, you can heal me and make me clean."

Jesus reached out and touched him. "I am willing," he said. "Be healed!" And instantly the leprosy disappeared.

Then Jesus instructed him not to tell anyone what had happened. He said, "Go to the priest and let him examine you. Take along the offering required in the law of Moses for those who have been healed of leprosy. This will be a public testimony that you have been cleansed."

But despite Jesus' instructions, the report of his power spread even faster, and vast crowds came to hear him preach and to be healed of their diseases.

Luke 5:12-15 NLT

Jesus realised what was going on in their minds and spoke straight to them.

"Why must you argue like this in your minds? Which do you suppose is easier—to say, 'Your sins are forgiven' or to say, 'Get up and walk'? But to make you realise that the Son of Man has full authority on earth to forgive sins—I tell you," he said to the man who was paralysed, "get up, pick up your bed and go home!"

Instantly the man sprang to his feet before their eyes, picked up the bedding on which he used to lie, and went off home, praising God. Sheer amazement gripped every man present,

and they praised God and said in awed voices,

"We have seen incredible things today."

Luke 5:22-26 Phillips

And it came to pass also on another sabbath, that he entered into the synagogue and taught: and there was a man whose right hand was withered.

And the scribes and Pharisees watched him, whether he would heal on the sabbath day; that they might find an accusation against him.

But he knew their thoughts, and said to the man which had the withered hand, Rise up, and stand forth in the midst. And he arose and stood forth.

Then said Jesus unto them, I will ask you one thing; Is it lawful on the sabbath days to do good, or to do evil? to save life, or to destroy it?

And looking round about upon them all, he said unto the man, Stretch forth thy hand. And he did so: and his hand was restored whole as the other.

Luke 6:6-10

He went down with them and stood on a level place. A large crowd of his disciples was there and a great number of people from all over Judea, from Jerusalem, and from the coastal region around Tyre and Sidon,

who had come to hear him and to be healed of their diseases. Those troubled by impure spirits were cured,

and the people all tried to touch him, because power was coming from him and healing them all.

Luke 6:17-19 NIV

When Jesus finished saying all these things to

the people, he went to Capernaum.

There was an army officer who had a servant who was very important to him. The servant was so sick he was nearly dead.

When the officer heard about Jesus, he sent some Jewish elders to him to ask Jesus to come and heal his servant.

The men went to Jesus and begged him, saying, "This officer is worthy of your help.

He loves our people, and he built us a synagogue."

So Jesus went with the men. He was getting near the officer's house when the officer sent friends to say, "Lord, don't trouble yourself, because I am not worthy to have you come into my house.

That is why I did not come to you myself. But you only need to command it, and my servant will be healed.

"I, too, am a man under the authority of others, and I have soldiers under my command. I tell one soldier, 'Go,' and he goes. I tell another soldier, 'Come,' and he comes. I say to my servant, 'Do this,' and my servant does it."

When Jesus heard this, he was amazed. Turning to the crowd that was following him, he said, "I tell you, this is the greatest faith I have found anywhere, even in Israel."

Those who had been sent to Jesus went back to the house where they found the servant in good health.

Luke 7:1-10 NCV

Soon afterward Jesus went with his disciples to the village of Nain, and a large crowd followed him.

A funeral procession was coming out as he approached the village gate. The young man who had died was a widow's only son, and a large crowd from the village was with her.

When the Lord saw her, his heart overflowed with compassion. "Don't cry!" he said.

Then he walked over to the coffin and touched it, and the bearers stopped. "Young man," he said, "I tell you, get up."

Then the dead boy sat up and began to talk! And Jesus gave him back to his mother.

Luke 7:11-15 NLT

When the men came to Jesus, they said, "John the Baptist sent us to you to ask, 'Are you the one who is to come, or should we expect someone else?'"

At that very time Jesus cured many who had diseases, sicknesses and evil spirits, and gave sight to many who were blind.

So he replied to the messengers, "Go back and

report to John what you have seen and heard: The blind receive sight, the lame walk, those who have leprosy are cleansed, the deaf hear, the dead are raised, and the good news is proclaimed to the poor.

Blessed is anyone who does not stumble on account of me."

Luke 7:20-23 NIV

A woman was in the crowd who had been bleeding for twelve years, but no one was able to heal her.

She came up behind Jesus and touched the edge of his coat, and instantly her bleeding stopped.

Then Jesus said, "Who touched me?"

When all the people said they had not touched him, Peter said, "Master, the people are all around you and are pushing against you."

But Jesus said, "Someone did touch me, because I felt power go out from me."

When the woman saw she could not hide, she came forward, shaking, and fell down before Jesus. While all the people listened, she told why she had touched him and how she had been instantly healed.

Jesus said to her, "Dear woman, you are made well because you believed. Go in peace."

Luke 8:43-48 NCV

While he was still speaking to her, a messenger arrived from the Jairus' home with the news that the little girl was dead. "She's gone," he told her father; "there's no use troubling the Teacher now."

But when Jesus heard what had happened, he said to the father, "Don't be afraid! Just trust me, and she'll be all right."

When they arrived at the house Jesus wouldn't let anyone into the room except Peter, James, John and the little girl's father and mother.

The home was filled with mourning people, but he said, "Stop the weeping! She isn't dead; she is only asleep!" This brought scoffing and laughter, for they all knew she was dead.

Then he took her by the hand and called, "Get up, little girl!" And at that moment her life returned and she jumped up! "Give her something to eat!" he said. Her parents were overcome with happiness, but Jesus insisted that they not tell anyone the details of what had happened.

Luke 8:49-56 TLB

Then he called his twelve disciples together, and gave them power and authority over all devils, and to cure diseases.

And he sent them to preach the kingdom of

God, and to heal the sick.

And they departed, and went through the towns, preaching the gospel, and healing every where.

Luke 9: 1-2,6

But the crowds learned about it and followed him. He welcomed them and spoke to them about the kingdom of God, and healed those who needed healing.

Luke 9:11 NIV

Behold, I give you the authority to trample on serpents and scorpions, and over all the power of the enemy, and nothing shall by any means hurt you.

Luke 10:19 NKJV

And a woman was there who had been crippled by a spirit for eighteen years. She was bent over and could not straighten up at all.

When Jesus saw her, he called her forward and said to her, "Woman, you are set free from your infirmity."

Then he put his hands on her, and immediately she straightened up and praised God.

Indignant because Jesus had healed on the Sabbath, the synagogue leader said to the people, "There are six days for work. So come and be healed on those days, not on the Sabbath."

The Lord answered him, "You hypocrites! Doesn't each of you on the Sabbath untie your ox or donkey from the stall and lead it out to give it water?

Then should not this woman, a daughter of Abraham, whom Satan has kept bound for eighteen long years, be set free on the Sabbath day from what bound her?"

When he said this, all his opponents were humiliated, but the people were delighted with all the wonderful things he was doing.

Luke 13:11-17 NIV

One Sabbath day Jesus went to eat dinner in the home of a leader of the Pharisees, and the people were watching him closely.

There was a man there whose arms and legs were swollen.

Jesus asked the Pharisees and experts in religious law, "Is it permitted in the law to heal people on the Sabbath day, or not?"

When they refused to answer, Jesus touched the sick man and healed him and sent him away.

Luke 14:1-4 NLT

And it came to pass, as he went to Jerusalem,

that he passed through the midst of Samaria and Galilee.

And as he entered into a certain village, there met him ten men that were lepers, which stood afar off:

And they lifted up their voices, and said, Jesus, Master, have mercy on us.

And when he saw them, he said unto them, Go shew yourselves unto the priests. And it came to pass, that, as they went, they were cleansed.

And one of them, when he saw that he was healed, turned back, and with a loud voice glorified God,

and fell down on his face at his feet, giving him thanks: and he was a Samaritan.

And Jesus answering said, Were there not ten cleansed? but where are the nine?

There are not found that returned to give glory to God, save this stranger.

And he said unto him, Arise, go thy way: thy faith hath made thee whole.

Luke 17:11-19

Then, as he was approaching Jericho, it happened that there was a blind man sitting by the roadside, begging. He heard the crowd passing and enquired what it was all about.

And they told him, "Jesus the man from Nazareth is going past you." So he shouted out, "Jesus, Son of David, have pity on me!"

Those who were in front tried to hush his cries. But that made him call out all the more, "Son of David, have pity on me!"

So Jesus stood quite still and ordered the man to be brought to him. And when he was quite close, he said to him, "What do you want me to do for you?" "Lord, make me see again," he cried.

"You can see again! Your faith has cured you,"

returned Jesus. And his sight was restored at once, and he followed Jesus, praising God. All the people who saw it thanked God too.

Luke 18:35-43 Phillips

When those with him saw what was happening, they said, "Master, shall we fight?" One of them took a swing at the Chief Priest's servant and cut off his right ear.

Jesus said, "Let them be. Even in this." Then, touching the servant's ear, he healed him.

Luke 22:49-51 Message

So Jesus came again to Cana of Galilee where He had made the water wine. And there was a certain nobleman whose son was sick at Capernaum.

When he heard that Jesus had come out of Judea into Galilee, he went to Him and implored

Him to come down and heal his son, for he was at the point of death.

Then Jesus said to him, "Unless you people see signs and wonders, you will by no means believe."

The nobleman said to Him, "Sir, come down before my child dies!"

Jesus said to him, "Go your way; your son lives." So the man believed the word that Jesus spoke to him, and he went his way.

And as he was now going down, his servants met him and told him, saying, "Your son lives!"

Then he inquired of them the hour when he got better. And they said to him, "Yesterday at the seventh hour the fever left him."

So the father knew that it was at the same hour

in which Jesus said to him, "Your son lives." And

he himself believed, and his whole household.

John 4:46-53 NKJV

Jesus saith unto him, Rise, take up thy bed, and walk.

And immediately the man was made whole, and took up his bed, and walked: and on the same day was the sabbath.

John 5:8-9

The Spirit alone gives eternal life. Human effort accomplishes nothing. And the very words I have spoken to you are spirit and life.

John 6:63 NLT

And as Jesus passed by, he saw a man which was blind from his birth.

And his disciples asked him, saying, Master, who did sin, this man, or his parents, that he was born blind?

Jesus answered, Neither hath this man sinned, nor his parents: but that the works of God should be made manifest in him.

I must work the works of him that sent me, while it is day: the night cometh, when no man can work.

As long as I am in the world, I am the light of the world.

When he had thus spoken, he spat on the ground, and made clay of the spittle, and he anointed the eyes of the blind man with the clay,

and said unto him, Go, wash in the pool of Siloam, (which is by interpretation, Sent.) He went his way therefore, and washed, and came seeing.

The neighbours therefore, and they which before had seen him that he was blind, said,

Is not this he that sat and begged?

Some said, This is he: others said, He is like him: but he said, I am he.

Therefore said they unto him, How were thine eyes opened?

He answered and said, A man that is called Jesus made clay, and anointed mine eyes, and said unto me, Go to the pool of Siloam, and wash: and I went and washed, and I received sight.

John 9:1-11

The thief comes only in order to steal and kill and destroy. I came that they may have and enjoy life, and have it in abundance (to the full, till it overflows).

John 10:10 AMP

Now a man named Lazarus was sick. He was from Bethany, the village of Mary and her sister Martha.

(This Mary, whose brother Lazarus now lay sick, was the same one who poured perfume on the Lord and wiped his feet with her hair.)

So the sisters sent word to Jesus, "Lord, the one you love is sick."

When he heard this, Jesus said, "This sickness will not end in death. No, it is for God's glory so that God's Son may be glorified through it."

Now Jesus loved Martha and her sister and Lazarus.

So when he heard that Lazarus was sick, he stayed where he was two more days,

and then he said to his disciples, "Let us go back to Judea."

"But Rabbi," they said, "a short while ago the Jews there tried to stone you, and yet you are going back?"

Jesus answered, "Are there not twelve hours of daylight? Anyone who walks in the daytime will not stumble, for they see by this world's light.

It is when a person walks at night that they stumble, for they have no light."

After he had said this, he went on to tell them, "Our friend Lazarus has fallen asleep; but I am going there to wake him up."

His disciples replied, "Lord, if he sleeps, he will get better."

Jesus had been speaking of his death, but his disciples thought he meant natural sleep.

So then he told them plainly, "Lazarus is dead, and for your sake I am glad I was not there, so that you may believe. But let us go to him."

Then Thomas (also known as Didymus) said to the rest of the disciples, "Let us also go, that we may die with him."

On his arrival, Jesus found that Lazarus had already been in the tomb for four days.

Now Bethany was less than two miles from

Jerusalem,

and many Jews had come to Martha and Mary to comfort them in the loss of their brother.

When Martha heard that Jesus was coming, she went out to meet him, but Mary stayed at home.

"Lord," Martha said to Jesus, "if you had been here, my brother would not have died.

But I know that even now God will give you whatever you ask."

Jesus said to her, "Your brother will rise again."

Martha answered, "I know he will rise again in the resurrection at the last day."

Jesus said to her, "I am the resurrection and the life. The one who believes in me will live, even though they die;

and whoever lives by believing in me will never die. Do you believe this?"

"Yes, Lord," she replied, "I believe that you are

the Messiah, the Son of God, who is to come into the world."

After she had said this, she went back and called her sister Mary aside. "The Teacher is here," she said, "and is asking for you."

When Mary heard this, she got up quickly and went to him.

Now Jesus had not yet entered the village, but was still at the place where Martha had met him.

When the Jews who had been with Mary in the house, comforting her, noticed how quickly she got up and went out, they followed her, supposing she was going to the tomb to mourn there.

When Mary reached the place where Jesus was and saw him, she fell at his feet and said, "Lord, if you had been here, my brother would not have died."

When Jesus saw her weeping, and the Jews who had come along with her also weeping, he was deeply moved in spirit and troubled.

"Where have you laid him?" he asked. "Come and see, Lord," they replied.

Jesus wept.

Then the Jews said, "See how he loved him!"

But some of them said, "Could not he who opened the eyes of the blind man have kept this man from dying?"

Jesus, once more deeply moved, came to the tomb. It was a cave with a stone laid across the entrance.

"Take away the stone," he said.

"But, Lord," said Martha, the sister of the dead man, "by this time there is a bad odor, for he has been there four days."

Then Jesus said, "Did I not tell you that if you believe, you will see the glory of God?"

So they took away the stone. Then Jesus looked up and said, "Father, I thank you that you have heard me. I knew that you always hear me, but I said this for the benefit of the people standing here, that they may believe that you sent me."

When he had said this, Jesus called in a loud voice, "Lazarus, come out!"

The dead man came out, his hands and feet wrapped with strips of linen, and a cloth around his face. Jesus said to them, "Take off the grave clothes and let him go."

John 11:1-44 NIV

And if you ask for anything in my name, I will do it for you so that the Father's glory will be shown through the Son.

If you ask me for anything in my name, I will do it.

John 14: 13-14 NCV

If you abide in Me, and My words abide in you,

ask whatever you wish, and it will be done for you.

John 15:7 NASB

In that day you will not question Me about anything. Truly, truly, I say to you, if you ask the Father for anything in My name, He will give it to you.

Until now you have asked for nothing in My name; ask and you will receive, so that your joy may be made full.

John 16: 23-24 NASB

Now Peter and John were going up to the temple at the ninth hour, the hour of prayer.

And a man who had been lame from his mother's womb was being carried along, whom they used to set down every day at the gate of the temple which is called Beautiful, in order to beg alms of those who were entering the temple.

When he saw Peter and John about to go into the temple, he began asking to receive alms.

But Peter, along with John, fixed his gaze on him and said, "Look at us!"

And he began to give them his attention, expecting to receive something from them.

But Peter said, "I do not possess silver and gold, but what I do have I give to you: In the name of Jesus Christ the Nazarene—walk!"

And seizing him by the right hand, he raised him up; and immediately his feet and his ankles were strengthened.

With a leap he stood upright and began to walk; and he entered the temple with them, walking and leaping and praising God.

And on the basis of faith in His name, it is the name of Jesus which has strengthened this man whom you see and know; and the faith which comes through Him has given him this perfect health in the presence of you all.

Acts 3:1-8, 16 NASB

Then Peter, filled with the Holy Spirit, said to them: "Rulers and elders of the people!

If we are being called to account today for an act of kindness shown to a man who was lame and are being asked how he was healed,

then know this, you and all the people of Israel: It is by the name of Jesus Christ of Nazareth, whom you crucified but whom God raised from the dead, that this man stands before you healed."

Acts. 4:8-10 NIV

And by the hands of the apostles were many signs and wonders wrought among the people; (and they were all with one accord in Solomon's porch.

And of the rest durst no man join himself to them: but the people magnified them.

And believers were the more added to the Lord, multitudes both of men and women.)

Insomuch that they brought forth the sick into the streets, and laid them on beds and couches, that at the least the shadow of Peter passing by might overshadow some of them.

There came also a multitude out of the cities round about unto Jerusalem, bringing sick folks, and them which were vexed with

unclean spirits: and they were healed every one.

Acts 5:12-16

And Stephen, full of faith and power, did great

wonders and miracles among the people.

Acts 6:8

Philip, for example, went to the city of Samaria and told the people there about the Messiah.

Crowds listened intently to Philip because they were eager to hear his message and see the miraculous signs he did.

Many evil spirits were cast out, screaming as they left their victims. And many who had been paralyzed or lame were healed.

So there was great joy in that city.

Acts 8:5-8 NLT

Now it happened that Peter, in the course of travelling about among them all, came to God's people living at Lydda. There he found a man called Aeneas who had been bed-ridden for eight years through paralysis. Peter said to him

"Aeneas, Jesus Christ heals you! Get up and make your bed."

He got to his feet at once. And all those who lived in Lydda and Sharon saw him and turned to the Lord.

Acts 9:32-35 Phillips

How God anointed Jesus of Nazareth with the Holy Ghost and with power: who went about doing good, and healing all that were oppressed of the devil; for God was with him.

Acts 10:38

In Lystra there sat a man who was lame. He had been that way from birth and had never walked.

He listened to Paul as he was speaking. Paul looked directly at him, saw that he had faith to be healed and called out, "Stand up on your feet!" At that, the man jumped up and began to walk.

Acts 14:8-10 NIV

And God did unusual and extraordinary miracles by the hands of Paul,

so that handkerchiefs or towels or aprons which had touched his skin were carried away and put upon the sick, and their diseases left them and the evil spirits came out of them.

Acts 19:11-12 AMP

And it came to pass, that the father of Publius lay sick of a fever and of a bloody flux: to whom Paul entered in, and prayed, and laid his hands on him, and healed him.

So when this was done, others also, which had

diseases in the island, came, and were healed:

Acts 28:8-9

As it is written: "I have made you a father of many nations." He is our father in the sight of God, in whom he believed—the God who gives life to the dead and calls into being things that were not.

Against all hope, Abraham in hope believed and so became the father of many nations, just as it had been said to him, "So shall your off-spring be."

Without weakening in his faith, he faced the fact that his body was as good as dead—since he was about a hundred years old—and that Sarah's womb was also dead.

Yet he did not waver through unbelief regarding the promise of God, but was strengthened in his faith and gave glory to God, being fully

persuaded that God had power to do what he
had promised.

Romans 4:17-21 NIV

But if the Spirit of him that raised up Jesus
from the dead dwell in you, he that raised up
Christ from the dead shall also quicken your
mortal bodies by his Spirit that dwelleth in you.

Therefore, brethren, we are debtors, not to the
flesh, to live after the flesh.

For if ye live after the flesh, ye shall die: but if
ye through the Spirit do mortify the deeds of the
body, ye shall live.

Romans 8:11-13

For the creation was subjected to frustration,
not by its own choice, but by the will of the one
who subjected it, in hope

And he who searches our hearts knows the

mind of the Spirit, because the Spirit intercedes for God's people in accordance with the will of God.

Romans 8:20,27 NIV

Now about the gifts of the Spirit, brothers and sisters, I do not want you to be uninformed.

You know that when you were pagans, somehow or other you were influenced and led astray to mute idols.

Therefore I want you to know that no one who is speaking by the Spirit of God says, "Jesus be cursed," and no one can say, "Jesus is Lord," except by the Holy Spirit.

There are different kinds of gifts, but the same Spirit distributes them.

There are different kinds of service, but the same Lord.

There are different kinds of working, but in all

of them and in everyone it is the same God at work.

Now to each one the manifestation of the Spirit is given for the common good.

To one there is given through the Spirit a message of wisdom, to another a message of knowledge by means of the same Spirit,

to another faith by the same Spirit, to another gifts of healing by that one Spirit,

to another miraculous powers, to another prophecy, to another distinguishing between spirits, to another speaking in different kinds of tongues, and to still another the interpretation of tongues.

All these are the work of one and the same Spirit, and he distributes them to each one, just as he determines.

I Corinthians 12:1-11 NIV

And God has appointed these in the church:

first apostles, second prophets, third teachers, after that miracles, then gifts of healings, helps, administrations, varieties of tongues.

Are all apostles? Are all prophets? Are all teachers? Are all workers of miracles?

Do all have gifts of healings? Do all speak with tongues? Do all interpret?

But earnestly desire the best gifts. And yet I show you a more excellent way.

1 Corinthians 12:28-31 NKJV

We are human, but we don't wage war as humans do.

We use God's mighty weapons, not worldly weapons, to knock down the strongholds of human reasoning and to destroy false arguments.

We destroy every proud obstacle that keeps people from knowing God. We capture their rebellious thoughts and teach them to obey Christ.

2 Corinthians 10:3-5 NLT

For though we live in the world, we do not wage war as the world does.

The weapons we fight with are not the weapons of the world. On the contrary, they have divine power to demolish strongholds.

We demolish arguments and every pretension that sets itself up against the knowledge of God, and we take captive every thought to make it obedient to Christ.

2 Corinthians 10:3-5 NIV

Christ hath redeemed us from the curse of the law, being made a curse for us: for it is written, Cursed is every one that hangeth on a tree:

That the blessing of Abraham might come on the Gentiles through Jesus Christ; that we might receive the promise of the Spirit through faith.

And if ye be Christ's, then are ye Abraham's seed, and heirs according to the promise

Galatians 3: 13-14, 29

Children, obey your parents because you be-long to the Lord, for this is the right thing to do.

"Honor your father and mother." This is the first commandment with a promise:

If you honor your father and mother, "things will go well for you, and you will have a long life on the earth."

Ephesians 6:1-3 NLT

In conclusion, be strong in the Lord [be em-powered through your union with Him]; draw your strength from Him [that strength which His boundless might provides].

Put on God's whole armor [the armor of a heavy-armed soldier which God supplies], that you may be able successfully to stand up against [all] the strategies and the deceits of the devil.

For we are not wrestling with flesh and blood [contending only with physical opponents], but against the despotisms, against the powers, against [the master spirits who are] the world rulers of this present darkness, against the spirit forces of wickedness in the heavenly (supernatural) sphere.

Therefore put on God's complete armor, that you may be able to resist and stand your ground on the evil day [of danger], and, having done all [the crisis demands], to stand [firmly in your place].

Stand therefore [hold your ground], having tightened the belt of truth around your loins and having put on the breastplate of integrity and of moral rectitude and right standing with God,

and having shod your feet in preparation [to

face the enemy with the firm-footed stability, the promptness, and the readiness produced by the good news] of the Gospel of peace.

Lift up over all the [covering] shield of saving faith, upon which you can quench all the flaming missiles of the wicked [one].

And take the helmet of salvation and the sword that the Spirit wields, which is the Word of God.

Pray at all times (on every occasion, in every season) in the Spirit, with all [manner of] prayer and entreaty.

To that end keep alert and watch with strong purpose and perseverance, interceding in behalf of all the saints (God's consecrated people).

Ephesians 6:10-18 AMP

Being confident of this very thing, that He who has begun a good work in you will complete it until the day of Jesus Christ;

Philippians 1:6 NKJV

Let this mind be in you which was also in Christ Jesus,

who, being in the form of God, did not consider it robbery to be equal with God,

but made Himself of no reputation, taking the form of a bondservant, and coming in the likeness of men.

And being found in appearance as a man, He humbled Himself and became obedient to the point of death, even the death of the cross.

Therefore God also has highly exalted Him and given Him the name which is above every name,

that at the name of Jesus every knee should bow, of those in heaven, and of those on earth,

and of those under the earth,

and that every tongue should confess that Jesus Christ is Lord, to the glory of God the Father.

Philippians 2:5-11 NKJV

And the very God of peace sanctify you wholly; and I pray God your whole spirit and soul and body be preserved blameless unto the coming of our Lord Jesus Christ.

1 Thessalonians 5:23

But women will be saved through childbearing if they continue in faith, love and holiness with propriety.

1 Timothy 2;15 NIV

Since we have a great high priest, Jesus the Son of God, who has gone into heaven, let us hold on to the faith we have.

For our high priest is able to understand our weaknesses. He was tempted in every way that we are, but he did not sin.

Let us, then, feel very sure that we can come before God's throne where there is grace. There we can receive mercy and grace to help us when we need it.

Hebrews 4:14-16 NCV

Then you will not become spiritually dull and indifferent. Instead, you will follow the example of those who are going to inherit God's promises because of their faith and endurance.

For example, there was God's promise to Abraham. Since there was no one greater to

swear by, God took an oath in his own name, saying:

"I will certainly bless you, and I will multiply your descendants beyond number."

Hebrews 6:12-14 NLT

Let us hold fast the profession of our faith without wavering; (for he is faithful that promised;)...

Hebrews 10:23

Therefore do not cast away your confidence, which has great reward.

For you have need of endurance, so that after you have done the will of God, you may receive the promise:

Hebrews 10:35-36 NKJV

But without faith it is impossible to please him: for he that cometh to God must believe that he is, and that he is a rewarder of them that diligently seek him.

Hebrews 11:6

Look after each other so that none of you fails

to receive the grace of God. Watch out that no poisonous root of bitterness grows up to trouble you, corrupting many.

Hebrews 12:15 NLT

Jesus Christ is the same yesterday, today, and forever.

Hebrews 13:8 NKJV

Is anyone among you in trouble? Let them pray. Is anyone happy? Let them sing songs of praise.

Is anyone among you sick? Let them call the elders of the church to pray over them and anoint them with oil in the name of the Lord.

And the prayer offered in faith will make the sick person well; the Lord will raise them up.

If they have sinned, they will be forgiven.

Therefore confess your sins to each other and

pray for each other so that you may be healed. The prayer of a righteous person is powerful and effective.

James 5:13-16 NIV

He personally carried the load of our sins in his own body when he died on the cross, so that we can be finished with sin and live a good life from now on. For his wounds have healed ours!

1 Peter 2:24 TLB

He Himself bore our sins in His body on the cross, so that we might die to sin and live to righteousness; for by His wounds you were healed.

1 Peter 2:24 NASB

In the same way, you who are younger, submit yourselves to your elders. All of you, clothe yourselves with humility toward one another, because, "God opposes the proud but shows favor to the humble."

Humble yourselves, therefore, under God's mighty hand, that he may lift you up in due time.

Cast all your anxiety on him because he cares for you.

Be alert and of sober mind. Your enemy the devil prowls around like a roaring lion looking for someone to devour.

Resist him, standing firm in the faith, because you know that the family of believers throughout the world is undergoing the same kind of sufferings.

And the God of all grace, who called you to his eternal glory in Christ, after you have suffered a little while, will himself restore you and make you strong, firm and steadfast.

1 Peter 5:5-10 NIV

You, dear children, are from God and have

overcome them, because the one who is in you is greater than the one who is in the world.

1 John 4:4 NIV

And we are confident that he hears us whenever we ask for anything that pleases him.

And since we know he hears us when we make our requests, we also know that he will give us what we ask for.

1 John 5:14-15 NLT

Beloved, I wish above all things that thou mayest prosper and be in health, even as thy soul prospereth.

3 John 2:1 KJV

My heartfelt prayer for you, my very dear

friend, is that you may be as healthy and pros
perous in every way are you are in soul.

3 John 2:1 Phillips

And they overcame him by the blood of the
Lamb, and by the word of their testimony.

Revelation 12:11

PRAYER OF SALVATION

God loves you—no matter who you are, no matter what your past. God loves you so much that He gave His one and only begotten Son for you. The Bible tells us that "…whoever believes in Him shall not perish but have eternal life" (John 3:16 NIV). Jesus laid down His life and rose again so that we could spend eternity with Him in heaven and experience His absolute best on earth. If you would like to receive Jesus into your life, say the following prayer out loud and mean it from your heart.

Heavenly Father, I come to You admitting that I am a sinner. Right now, I choose to turn away from sin, and I ask You to cleanse me of all unrighteousness. I believe that Your Son, Jesus, died on the cross to take away my sins. I also believe that He rose again from the dead so that I might be forgiven of my sins and made righteous through faith in Him. I call upon the name of Jesus Christ to be the Savior and Lord of my life. Jesus, I choose to follow You and ask that You fill me with the power of the Holy Spirit. I declare that right now I am a child of God. I am free from sin and full of the righteousness of God. I am saved in Jesus' name. Amen.

If you prayed this prayer to receive Jesus Christ as your Savior for the first time, please contact us on the Web at **www.harrisonhouse.com** to receive a free book.

Or you may write to us at

Harrison House • P.O. Box 35035 • Tulsa, Oklahoma 74153

Fast. Easy. Convenient.

For the latest Harrison House product information and author news, look no further than your computer. All the details on our powerful, life-changing products are just a click away. New releases, E-mail subscriptions, testimonies, monthly specials—find it all in one place. Visit harrisonhouse.com today!

harrisonhouse

The Harrison House Vision

Proclaiming the truth and the power
Of the Gospel of Jesus Christ
With excellence;

Challenging Christians to
Live victoriously,
Grow spiritually,
Know God intimately.